The Treekeeper's Tale

For Brian

Also by Pascale Petit

Icefall Climbing

Heart of a Deer

Tying the Song (Co-edited with Mimi Khalvati)

The Zoo Father

El Padre Zoológico/The Zoo Father

The Huntress

The Wounded Deer

Pascale Petit
The Treekeeper's Tale

SEREN

Seren is the book imprint of
Poetry Wales Press Ltd.
57 Nolton Street, Bridgend, Wales, CF31 3AE
www.serenbooks.com

ISBN 978-1-85411-471-6

A CIP record for this title is available from the British Library.

The publisher acknowledges the financial assistance of
the Welsh Books Council.

Cover art by the author – 'Treekeeper' (1987).
Back cover portrait of the author by Kitty Sullivan.

Printed in Palatino by 4edge Limited, Hockley.

Contents

The Treekeeper's Tale

Afterlives

War Horse

The Chrysanthemum Lantern

The Treekeeper's Tale

The Treekeeper's Tale

I have set up house in the hollow trunk of a giant redwood.
My bed is a mat of pine needles. Cones drop their spirals

on my face as I sleep. I have the usual flying dreams.
But all I know when I wake is that this bark is my vessel

as I hurtle through space. Once, I was rocked in a cradle
carved from a coast redwood, its lullabies were my coracle.

I searched for that singing grove and became its guardian.
There are days when the wind plays each tree

like a new instrument in the forest-orchestra.
On wild nights mine is a flute. After years of solitude

I have started to hear its song. I lie staring at the stars
until the growth rings enclose me in hoops –

choirs of concentric colours, as if my tree is remembering
the music of the spheres. And I almost remember speaking

my first word, how it flew out of my mouth like a dove.
I have forgotten how another of my kind sounds.

Chandelier-Tree

I find myself staring at the spaces between
fronds, where pure blue plumes appear,
the air painting itself on my eye.

And I see how the trunk doesn't end
where a person can climb, but continues
to the redwood's true crown, sky-feathers

piercing the stratosphere, blue forest
on blue, some white with lace frills
of finest cirrus, before the wide canopy

of night, its invisible leaves
suddenly alert with stars – how they are
glimpses of the tree of light.

Exiled Elm

My comet-roots trail earth through the dark,
my trunk swarms with homeless insects

and from my starry crown seeds
scatter, searching for new worlds.

Creation of the Birds

after the painting by Remedios Varo

I paint birds from starlight.
The harder my art, the stronger their wings –

solar or lunar feathered, iris-barbed.
The ultrasonic syrinx,

drawn from my violin-brush,
starts to hum when I'm lonely.

I release them while still wet, their songs
liquid and light, not meant for base ears.

Even the nests they weave in our old forests
are harmonies – temporary mouths for our trees.

Restless, they embark on great migrations,
beat against the glass of earth's cage.

A Dawn Trail

Each day we come earlier, searching for that hush
    no freeway hum will shatter,

  when the morning wind blows all sound
    into the next creek

  and even our footsteps are muffled
    by a soundproof carpet.

Deeper into the silence we notice the flutter
    of dropping needles

  soft as feathers from the sky, and a pause
    in which we sense a presence,

  where we begin to see ourselves as part of the forest,
    the thought emerging

  like a white doe who keeps a shy distance,
    at home in the heart of the grove,

  before language, before the human tongue
    took root.

Portrait of a Coast Redwood Forest with Mandolin

When the first ray pierces my canvas
I breathe on its shaft, make solar music.
It's in these early hours of a painting's life
that my palette becomes a mandolin, its thumb-hole

a soundhole plucked by brushes. My eye
darts from foliage to fog. I try to paint
the deep notes of these ancients,
how the bass rises from their roots

and spirals round their rings
before bursting into saturated light.
There is lake-black and mud-brown
a loon-shape brings up from the river bed

like primordial clay; red dots to raise
from drums of resonating bark.
There are greys to draw down from the clouds
like masks for the tree-gods' faces,

lightning to cast over their crowns.
The way they stir just before a storm,
the crack that opens in the sky – my first view
of the thunder woods in their electric groves.

Uprooted Redwood

My crown once swayed above the stratosphere like a raft,
each pine-needle tuned to the stars.

You can hear my leaves humming
an infinite green fugue. It's as if dawn depends on it,

for ladders of light to be lowered through violet fog.
The sun paints an improvised harmony – crescents,

splashes, zigzags, a lemon lagoon. A blue blot explodes,
leaving a crater in the sky, cascades of rose roots.

Morning lies in the gorge, raw as ripped wood.

The University among the Redwoods, Santa Cruz

They're up there – the students, in their high halls,
sleeping among the redwoods, in the university of leaves.

The sky is a blue-bound volume of flickering
white pages they wake to – a morning mist

of evaporating inks. All night, a black bible
big as the universe writes star-scriptures.

The sequoias are illuminated manuscripts
through which to glimpse stories of our sun.

Their branches hum as tree-scholars take the morning
staircase down. On every floor they pass

another library of light, upper storeys where birds
sing hosannas, the hymn of canopy cascades,

sky-pools for the clouded salamander, the great
hanging gardens of the treetops. As the students

descend, they become heavier, they stumble
down the steps, for they have come to the middle region

where needles start to hiss as the breezes hush,
the zone of knotholes where stars have nested

in the night-tree's swaying mast. To the lower trunk
where scrolls are ash in smouldering fire-caves.

They crawl past zones of silence, those sawn-
through stadium-stumps, and they go to class.

Treesitter

Silence has small sounds I have learnt to listen to with my skin –
the sap's slow rise up three hundred feet of xylem. Here,

where the winds make harps of needle-plumes,
morning bathes me in musical mists. Below me, birds

stretch their wings in shivering shoals of green amber.
Beneath them, the fluted trunk plunges to an earth

I have not stepped on for two years. The first few months
of my treesit they tried scaring me out with choppers,

stopped me from sleeping with floodlights, air-horns, whistles.
But my mind grew a fireproof bark. One by one,

I have watched the great trees fall all around mine in the grove.
What I remember most is the moment the chainsaw

is switched off – that different silence, as if each
of my neighbour's leaves is holding its breath

before releasing a gasp – a trembling that spirals down
to the cut. Years reel as its rings just stand there shaking.

Nature Singer

The trees taught me to sing like a bird, pitch
my voice so high the notes nest in the canopy
before flying into your ears.

I can mimic the loon. My tremolo settling on Eel River
causes ripples to quiver and fan out –
a drowned soul could reappear from one of those rings
to haunt the attentive listener.

At full force, my voice can put out a flame.
I have learnt to do this from the mighty redwood
which knows how to hold fire without burning.
The lightning bolt strikes its heart and shatters.

Since I was a child I have heard the trees talking,
a green thunder that could crack bones
but descends softly, like falling leaves.

Osprey Nests

Sticks, seaweed, crosshatchings and slashes.
Toy sailboats, doormats, discarded rubber teat holders
from milking machines, TV antennas,
hula hoops, fish nets, rubber boots,
a broken bicycle tyre – worthless
unless put to use the birds agree.
A book called *Lucille, Bringer of Joy*;
various dried carcasses, derelict clothing.
A fondness for the shiny and artificial:
the fluorescent stuffing of an Easter basket
and large green garbage bags
that fly like flags off pirate ships.
Prize to the pair at Chapin Beach
who added a naked Barbie doll to their northeast wall.
At least a half dozen elaborate tunnels.
Sheer mass, dainty perfectionism.
More tall than wide,
weighing close to a ton.
Sanctuary word aeries
built higher each passing year.
Climb up into one for the winter – they support a man.

Redwood Canopy Explorer

I hang in the spaces between canopies
and when I pause for breath it hits me –
the total silence. Even my mental chatter
vanishes. Just me and these ancient beings
and the rain they filter from the fog
dripping on my glistening skin.
I glide in a wordless mist. All that holds me
to the spinning planet is a little rope.
I start to soar as if the needles sprouted feathers,
my muscles tensed for flight. And when I land
it's on a hanging garden of fern-mats
ninety metres high, to kneel on its altar.
Every dip into the chalice of a sky-pool
yields an unknown species. Everything is dawn-new.

Creation of the Trees

after the painting Harmony *by Remedios Varo*

I set the musical stave on my desk,
strung notes on its metal wires,
using fossils, shells, prisms, as quavers

and semiquavers, trying to make music
from matter. I summoned treasures
from the chest for so long

I thought it was bottomless, the source
of the rivers of sound that drove my world.
I longed for harmonies to grow the trees,

so the songs of their light would flood my studio.
The muse even lent a hand. She emerged
from the peeling wallpaper, her vellum-

wrinkled fingers moved the notes
until a faint prelude crept out.
The air vibrated like branches in a breeze.

I blew through the clef to add my breath
and the trees became a hovering forest. I composed
falling rain, dew-drip, the budding leaves.

Afterlives

The Second Husband

After what feels like two thousand years
    I find you under the permafrost.
I dig and dig until your twelve frozen horses
    spring up in their red felt masks and ibex horns.
You must have ridden each one to heaven

in your high headdress with its gold foil frieze
    of Celestial Mountains, your crest
of winged snow leopards and antlered wolves
    with eagle tines. When you ask me to stay
 I know this is the afterlife.

Two Golden Eagles

Saykhan

Holding Saykhan is unexpected as meeting you
after all those years on my own.
Here in the Tien Shan where it's minus twenty degrees,
with this sudden weight on my gauntlet,
I peer into tawny eyes, see the wolves he's killed,
swooping onto their napes to knock them down.
If he draws blood he'll attack but the glove
protects me from his talons and he bears
those jesses that bind him to me.
If he took off he'd lift me with him –
the way we rise into sheer air above the rolling steppe of our bed,
our wing-feathers icicles
while we glide through snow's embroidered sheets,
our faces cataracts of light.

Kukai

This time it's you holding a female golden eagle
and I'm her, gripping your hand through the gauntlet,
my hood pulled off as if for the hunt.
You've propped me on your arm for a photo
where we'll always be together.
You've noted my beak, my two-inch claws,
how piercing my eyesight is,
and how at home I am in this biting cold.
For the moment I trust you, even when
your fingers feel my wings, so that although tethered,
I start flying in my mind.
And when you follow on horseback to claim
my quarry, I let you believe it's yours.
I wait until you allow me to feed.

Frozen Horses

Twelve frozen corpses – one for each lonely year
sealed under the Altai Desert.

You came with your pickaxe and hacked them out.
You looked in my eyes and saw the graves inside –

twelve sacrificed horses with red saddles
and gold bridles, braided tails and tassels.

Tenderly, you thawed their birch bark beds
and proud manes, their reindeer masks

and antlers for flying to the after-world
from that Iron Age pit.

Unearthing my solitude, you glimpsed
its silver coat and pearl hooves, its pricked ears.

Siberian Ice Maiden

On my table is a mutton tail,
a bronze knife with wolf handle, jug of khoumis,
a translucent yak horn bowl.

My six horses lie near, their coats still
that chestnut sheen. They face east
in their gilt saddles with felt cushions
       stuffed with stag-hair,
bridles covered with gold leaf.

My coffin is carved from a single larch log
and curves like a cradle. Four copper nails
seal it shut, and on the sides, leather reindeer fly.

Open my lid to a block of milky white ice.
Dismayed my cocoon is opaque,
your pace slackens.

Melt me. Heat buckets with blowtorches to pour
boiling water into my casket,
       cup by careful cup,
until the scent of coriander is released.

At night you dream of gouged eyes,
the sockets stuffed with fur.

Each day you stand in freezing water
as the smell of wet wool gets stronger
and you glimpse gold flecks in the ice.

Your arms move as if in trance
as I emerge from my two-thousand-year
       sleep,
curled on my left side,
my cheek nestled against the pillow.

Only patches of my face remain.
My hair has been shaved, a hole cut in my skull

to insert incense and pine cones
            instead of a brain,
the gash sewn with sinew.

I am alone in my Tree of Life headdress
            on its larch frame.
Tien Shan snow leopards, gold birds, a griffin,
            perch on its branches.
A quiver and bow hang from the apex.

Pull back the marten fur blanket to view my necklace
            of carved camels.
Lift the blouse from my shoulder to find flesh
tattooed a deep midnight blue –
a frieze of deer-horses with blossoming horns.

My hands are intact,
the thumbs dyed with swirling indigo antlers that break into
                                                    flower
            when you touch them.

The curves of my breasts are soft
            as the day I was buried,
my skin yellow from tannins.

Behind my bent knees a red pouch
holds my brass mirror, horsehair brush, iron eye-pencil.
You trace long incisions in my back, belly and limbs
            where my organs and muscles were removed,
peat, bark and sedge packed in their place.

That early spring, when I died young on the Pasture of Heaven
I was wearing this crimson blouse of wild silk,
this thick wool and camel hair skirt,
white felt stockings, a belt,
these still supple thigh-high riding boots to protect my skin
            from chaffing against the saddle –
all made it
            through the centuries unscathed.

I was preserved until the ground thawed enough
to bury me in the Altai, high up
where only ibex climb and eagles nest
        so I could reach the afterlife
on the backs of my horses.

                                    Now
I am displayed in this museum, my clothes
and sacred ornaments on mannequins behind glass,
        my body naked.

Salmon

The moon was coming up one side of the river
and the sun was setting on the other
when a huge salmon leapt

from the shock of whitewater. On his left flank
his scales shimmered with moonlight,
on his right they blazed with sun.

He seemed to hang there in the air
in pyjamas of pearl and ash,
half a wedding-suit of rosefire.

I thought of you asleep in the cabin
and rushed home to look
as sunset's last rays costumed your back

through one window, and the full moon
robed your chest through the other. You jumped
as if you'd leapt out of yourself

and were heading upstream. For a moment
you hung there, half out of your skin,
your body lost in the shadows.

Baby Moon

We've hung a baby moon in a birdcage
from our bedroom ceiling.

We climb a silver birch ladder
to feed her star gruel.

She cries a lot, wants the window left open
so a breeze will rock her.

Each month she grows thin and vanishes.
When she's full, her light floods our bed.

We lie under her like two squid,
our skins flickering with seas.

Atlas Moth

This giant atlas moth's broad wings
could be the map of China.

Here are two Great Walls. And there
on the Manchurian tip of each forewing

are dragon heads to scare off predators.
But what are those windows in the map,

where crystal scales let in the light?
As if earth's skin has windows

and at certain times of the evening
they open. The newly emerged atlas

perches on my hand, and it trembles –
like a new world, warming up for its first flight.

Slipper Orchids of China

At the foot of Yellow Mountain I find a slipper orchid
crouching like a toad.

No three inch golden lotus, the pouch is smaller,
flecked maroon-black like a Ming Dynasty grave shoe –

So many empty moccasins from women quiet
as petals, released from their bonds.

Hieroglyph Moth

When the white ermine wings
opened at night

like a book of frost
        smoking in the dark,

I understood the colours of vowels
painted on moth fur –

the black, red, saffron signs
of a new language.

Antennae grew from my forehead,
my tongue was restless in its chrysalis.

I felt lift-off
        as if my bones had melted.
I stepped out into the snow –

not even an exoskeleton to protect me
in this strange country.

Escape

I pushed headfirst into the light
through the nine circles of your cervix,

then rested, my face free of you.
You gripped my shoulders.

You were a stone I had to crawl out of.
But there was this air I wanted to breathe,

clouds of it floating in the colour-room
where cold voices cut my skin.

I must have been tunnelling for months,
planning escape-routes

in those new mazes of my brain.
There was a hole in my head

through which I could hear the stars singing.
The seal over my lips cracked

as I tried to sing back.
Angels drew out my legs

and washed you off me.
I was not yet your daughter. You

would never be my mother.
Those threats you whispered

as I lay helpless inside you
were in no mother tongue.

The moment my feet left you
I started to worship the world.

Moon Moths (in the Day Room)

She is just out of the cocoon of childhood,
her colours still wet,
when I bring the luna chrysalids.

I thread them into rows,
tie them over her scarred wrists.
They rattle when we gently shake them.

Only my mother can wear them –
moon charms are too dangerous
to be worn by the sane.

Only she can slit the silk cages
and draw out the cherubs that have died
during the great transformation,

their bullet-bodies closed,
their antennae bent back
over leather wing-stubs.

Those moths that have survived
take only a flash to emerge.
How she loves to see them

grow there on her palms,
from tiny flaps to gold archangels
with hind tips fluttering like comets.

She gazes at the quivering beings
as if holding her soul. For once
her hands stop shaking.

The Bee Mother

I want to go back now, through the buzzing darkness.
I want to go into that humming hive awake,
wearing the net curtain you called my veil.

I want to walk down childhood's garden
as that girl who married her mother,
through the marguerite bed

to that nest, where my bee-queen lies
deep in her brood chamber.
I want to see the honeycomb of your mind.

I want to look into your compound eyes
where I'm reflected as an angry swarm.
I want to be that daughter whose mother has stung her

because she's a rival,
who's still pumping venom into her.
I want to be that childless worker

who dared to sting back, shreds
of my torn abdomen hanging off you
as I leave my stinger behind.

I have cleaned the window of my self until I gleam.
I want you to see how radiant I am
on this, my wedding day.

With all the love I now know,
I want to brush the halo of your hair
and mend the delicate rays of your wings.

I'll place royal jelly in your coffin
for your last flight
and close the moonlit petals of your face.

My Larzac Childhood

She lies in her daybed, her brown sheets rustling with earthworms,
her beetle-carapace eye sockets staring up at me.

I trap stag beetles in a box and watch them battle like Maman's left
and right eyes.

I am always avoiding her gaze, and yet yearning for the blaze
behind her icicle-eyelashes.

I sit quietly as a stone, smelling aromatic mint mingled with wild
thyme, stab myself with brambles until my cries are louder than her
cicada-chants

and our furniture surfaces from the soil. The springs of her mattress
uncoil from the wall, and here, under the lintel of a root-door, lies
the mangled frame of that picture I hated.

I was raised in the Larzac, by a mistral-mother and a thistle-father.
Two years she shared her bed with this monster. Two years she was
the wind whetting his knife-sharpener spikes. His lips ground back
and forth on hers.

Her figleaf-hands wave to me from the top of the vineyard, where it
vanishes into a tangle of oak-impaled boar carcasses.

Then I follow the sunshine-freckled stream, to climb down the
knotted ladder into its deep bed and hop from one stepping-stone
to another, dodging the leaf roof.

My face turns like the Hourglass Nebula. The underwood-breathing,
eagle-shrieking, minnowed whirlpool of my mind brims like the
stream at full spate.

I love everything that tumbled from the plateau into crayfish pools –
their claws are the dead waving, beckoning me up to the cascade,
to shower under its silver shoals.

The drops shocking my skin seem to sprout feather-shafts as I fly
through the mossy past. And back into the sunglare, to dragonflies
magnified by noon,

the museums of their abdomens, wings opening like skylights of art galleries. I have spent my life trying to see these living palettes give birth to colour.

I love the sun-bronze kingfisher and mud-velvet water rat equally in their earth burrows.

I love the bear-bumblebee and tiger-hornet, the day frog and night toad, everything that teems where my giant shadow roams, while under Maman's gaze my child-shadow shrivels.

I used to haul water up from the stream for washing, and down from the source for drinking. I was always climbing up and down the steep terraces,

my childhood suspended between the rungs, over the adder-surprising, grass-snake-flashing paths, as I paused with my load.

I was always scrubbing the spider-infested walls of our stone cottage with hard brooms, filling the cracks with stones. Yet each night, star insects crawled in from their sky nests.

Peeping through the hole next to my pillow, I could see a wasps' nest galaxy, its queen laying double suns.

A constellation of white ants raided our larders, ate everything we didn't lock in the cupboard.

Black rats ran along time's warped rafters, dropped onto my face as I slept.

I saw the universe was a vineyard choking with brambles, patrolled by light year long praying mantises. I saw their straw-green helmets and Milky Way eyes.

What do you want from me? I asked them, and their telescope eyes peered into mine and spoke.

I scratch at Maman's dripstone encrusted cave-coffin, and weave a web of roots around it as if I could store her in my keepnet until I am strong enough to face her.

The south breeze caresses me as I walk from ridge to ridge. The Mediterranean gleams like a radiant corpse, waves of its skin rising into the air to become cirrus.

I am always at home, listening to the bone-voiced dead. I am always at my mother's grave, telling her everything.

Did she know that she carried a dragon, that when she breastfed me I drank her bile and stored it in my body to turn to fire later?

That when she made me speak, before my trembling voice obeyed her command, a firecloud escaped from my mouth to burn her face?

I was a silent and sullen child, deep as a well, magma boiling at its base. Getting me to talk was like drawing water and bringing up a lava bomb.

I call her and she rises, trailing a rain of roots and stalactites, like the stormcloud at the end of childhood's summer.

She sits with me at the table, a hulk of electric air; a river's catch, raised and suspended.

A whole farmhouse hovers in the gloom. In her thunderhead the gentle cows are trapped, their bells ringing.

Seven years I stayed silent. I would not talk to her storm-face or eclipse-hair, even that one night she softened, and I saw the lunar arcs on her brow.

I lay the table. The waxed cloth is printed with sunflowers and lavender, poppies and corn. The cicadas chant a grace. It is summer in our plates.

The wine is from our vineyard – a prehistoric vintage. The fruit is from our trees. I weeded them. I pruned them. The donkey carried water to them.

My plate spins and I start eating Catherine wheels. I drink the wine of newborn stars; sip cognac old as Centaurus.

The Reckless Sleeper

after René Magritte

You are lying in your alcove
with six treasures I buried with you –

a hand-mirror, a lit candle, a black hat,
an apple, a living bird and Maman's blue bow.

Wood grain surrounds you like
waves of REM dreaming.

The bow still smells of the evening
when you forced your hot candle

into the trembling bird of her sex.
The apple turns its unbitten cheek

towards me. The mirror also turns its back
as if to hide its face. The bowler

is the one she wore to marry you
in a man's funeral suit. You sleep on,

Papa, but the dream never changes.

Self-Portrait as the King Vulture's Bride

The morning I buried you there was a thick fog
like embalming fluid. I waited and waited
at the morgue – a low red building like an open wound.
You lay in your rough coffin, ice-cold,
with that burn-bruise, and I leant over
and kissed your cheek. It was rainbow-coloured
like a king vulture's – coral-rose, storm-purple,
some white hairs pushing through
like a hatchling's first plumage
or last night's stubble. You flickered from father
to vulture, and I flickered beside you.
My flight feathers whistled as I rode the thermals
to get closer. Dear baby Dad, dear bridegroom –
see how I was the first to arrive at the carcass.

Creation of the Himalayas

after the painting Embroidering Earth's Mantle *by Remedios Varo*

They say we are just embroiderers
but when we are working well, our tower turns
into burnished fire and the mantle flows
from our fingers, tumbling through the air
in loops of delight. There are always men
trapped in our weave. The sky calls their names
and they climb, trying to reach back
through the clouds to our blue fingers.
They glimpse us over the Tibetan Plateau,
our needles flashing like nimbus.
Each dancing thread and singing stitch
must be precisely placed in its matrix.
Here where there is no oxygen
and the cold stings like a furnace,
our eyes spin like constellations
as we sew tapestries on our stellar frames
and let them drop through the slits in the walls.
We who have no voice hear
the snow's musical swirl across matter,
sense through our fingertips
a face emerging from Khumbu Glacier.
We weigh nothing, and our cloth when it's new
weighs less than us before it sets in its stone cage.
We never tire, knowing that the folds
that form under great pressure spurt wings,
and Chomolungma grows higher each year, homesick.
We add temples around her base,
work harder, the earth pouring through our palms.

Machapuchere (Fishtail Mountain)

Waking in the Remember Lodge, I throw a glacier-cloak over my
nightie,
shock myself awake

to find Fishtail silhouetted against the night.
Machapuchere the unclimbable, ally of shamans

who hang spirit-traps over the rope bridge to protect their
children's school
from hail and avalanche,

who, in times of trouble, sing a mountain-chant
in stone-bass and ice-vowels, smoke swirling from their mouths,

as now my breath rises in dawn-drafts, up into eagle air
to be washed by the stars.

I am always on the flagstones of that mule path,
waiting for the accentor robin's morning mantra

before mud thunders down the landslide.
I will always climb until it goes quiet

and I can no longer hear Modi River's roar,
just to watch lightning skein the gorge in flash-waterfalls.

Yesterday I trekked almost as far as Ghandruk through monsoon.
The trail was a broken cascade.

Just before sunset, a hole cleared in the clouds, unveiled
the double dagger peaks,

a hole jagged as Shiva's third eye, which he may open
to incinerate the world.

The flanks gradually whiten in a morning-glory blue
and the rising sun lights up the first fin, snow blowing from the tip

until it catches fire.
And as I stand still as an unclimbed mountain, hour after hour,

each gully and glacier in the Annapurna Sanctuary emerging
                                                    from my
memory,
I see how the river leaps into the sky, returning to its source –

a Milky Way boiling with whirlpools and rapids; spiral mirror
that gets darker and slower the further down the valley it flows,

past tea-houses, straggling stalls, to the highway that winds back
                                        towards Pokhara.

The Hudson Remembers

From Riverside Drive, I stared at you
until I was in a trance.
And the trance-river was long, wide,
and glistened like a great tower
which reared into the sky.
I saw your waves were panes of glass
polished by the autumn rays.
I saw, along your length,
your windows unzipping –
splinters of plate glass stung my cheeks.
You were so bright and wrong,
as if our sun had plunged from his office
and was laid on a stretcher.
I heard a thundering in your bed
that was our star's throes.
Then I realised that your flowing
to the ocean was a falling
that would never end.
People inside you, on a hundred floors,
in your rooms, at your desks,
in your stairwells, your lifts,
in your corridors, swept by currents.
And they were breathing smoke
as if drowning in black water,
charred by flames of river-cold.
And your twin – East River –
also remembers, as it falls with you
into the Atlantic, where seabirds
dive into debris like airliners,
and the continental shelf drops away.
There, reams of scattered papers
float down into the abyss,
until all their addresses are erased.

Night Boat on Galilee

I board when the surface is calm
    as the lull before a symphony.

In that pause a lyre-lake
    mirrors the stars.

If I listen hard I almost hear a nocturne's opening chords
    as I float over earth's rift,

and in my net, a shoal of notes
    flap their tails.

My boat cradles me as a squall swoops
    from the Golan Heights

and plucks the roots of subterranean springs
    that feed the shrinking lake.

The woods of quiet are carob, willow, Aleppo pine,
    terebinth, tabor oak and cedar.

The two-thousand-year-old fishing vessel dredged from clay
    after a year of drought

was built from these – planks so waterlogged
    they would disintegrate in air.

I board that craft between destruction and repair,
    in the listening-lake Kinneret

where Jesus walked over two thousand strings
    of liquid harp,

summoning lightness from a breath of birdsong.
    I board my boat

as sound waves lap against the hull
    drawing Aeolian sighs

from the rings of the Tree of Life.
       And if this wreck is from a battle

I'll sing to the spirits of the trees
       which were felled to build it

until the leaves grow back on their branches
       and water rises up dry veins – enough for the world

to drink, for the water-music to stop all wars. I still my ears
       as the constellations tune their instruments.

War Horse

War Horse

after Franz Marc

Yesterday, I saw a horse die –
the most fiery but obedient white Pegasus

groaned in great pain like a human
wakened from a vivid dream.

Now he is a stinking corpse.
Nights, I sleep in the meadow.

When it's quiet, the stars open.
They are my flowers. Darling –

when you look at our garden,
think of me looking up at mine.

Have you seen the War-Comet?
Bigger than Halley's,

it follows us over the fields of France.
It has an icy mane.

Dispatch Rider

after Franz Marc

I ride a tower of blue horses
like a stained-glass window,
our haunches hard as lead crystal.

The sun shines through us onto the battlefield,
our veins reflecting as mountain streams
that the dead can bathe in.

I ride the brood mare of sapphire stallions.
I ride a herd of her colts right up to the front.
And after we have delivered our letter,

we leave, with our diamond eyes that cut
and our furnace manes,
our hooves heavier than cannons.

We clear the barbed wire fences.
We who carry the stars like weapons
in the cathedrals of our bodies,

leap over the trenches. Arrive
back in our stables – every glass pane
shivering and intact.

Blue Foal Dreaming

after Franz Marc

Here comes the green horse, his flanks
of fresh-mown lawn, his hooves
like sapling roots. Through a pause in the gunfire
he trots, over the mud, to nuzzle
the blue foal who lies dreaming. Is this
why horses were created? Who
will ride away on the cool cobalt back
of the woken foal? Who will grasp
his mane streaming with storms? Even
the wounded want to leap bareback. In one
bound, they'll reach the edge of the trenches,
where a red mare is giving birth
to a white colt with wings soft as drifts.

The Doves of Verdun

after Franz Marc

Their wingbones are rifles,
their feathers bayonets.

They carry grenade pins
instead of twigs in their beaks.

Their nests are explosions
of shrapnel and fuse wire.

One has laid its egg in my temple.
It hatches, just under the eaves of my fringe.

Bluish Fabulous Beast

after Franz Marc

This is the horse I will die on.
There'll be clouds on his blue coat

when shrapnel shrieks into me.
His whinny will stop the stars in their course.

I'll see the lightning in his neck
as he turns transparent.

Then I will fall, blessed
by the ambrosia of his sweat.

My body will brush his mane
as each hair-shaft breaks into flight.

The Trees Show their Rings,
the Animals their Veins

after Franz Marc

That clear night, I saw a new kind of painting
on a great black canvas. The moon hung low

as if conducting a colour symphony.

The animals offered their veins as violin strings.
The trees unwound their rings

for dressings to staunch the deepest wounds.

Stars choired over the front line
which flowered with musical notes.

For days afterwards, I carried the constellations
in my head like a fragrant nocturne.

The Chrysanthemum Lantern

Scapecat

after Zhou Zan

They hung him after a battle between two gangs of kids –
one side was called Eighth Route, the other Japanese Ghosts.
The fighting broke out behind the bleachery
and village storehouse, in May after wheat harvest.
The dung heap and thresher were their bunkers.
The wounded flung themselves into bales
and would forever smell hay in their nostrils.
Yet the battle always ended the same – the enemy
was beaten, and officers Matsumoto or Gumi arrested.
An old black cat was the last victim, captured
as he happened to pass by. They said his scream
was the enemy's death struggle and announced the lynching.

Jay

after Zhou Zan

I always heard their talk,
could translate it like Gong Ye-chang
who understood the language of birds.
One of the jays returned from a far journey,
full of herself, chattering about her adventures.
The other jays screeched at her, some believed
some doubted. They made such a racket
that the taleteller raised her voice, long and loud,
proudly at first, then sad
to have told her secrets. She was so tired,
refused to enlighten these fools.
And mum always criticised me, called me a burden of talking.
"Shut up Jay
you're too small, you can't even carry things."
But one day a jay fell
from the nest of sleep
and died under the locust tree,
her beak firmly closed, too young
to translate death's silence.

The chrysanthemum lantern is floating over me

after Zhai Yongming

A chrysanthemum lantern is floating towards me.
In the enveloping silence of pitch darkness –
a low murmur of children on the riverbank.
The lantern is so sheer a bird's shadow shows through it.

The children's chorus floats over with the lantern.
There's no fear, no pain,
only the lantern, the lightness of chrysanthemums
and the red glow of its candle.

A young girl also floats over –
a girl and her maids,
their hair up,
their luxurious clothes nothing but
silk, ribbons and buttons,
nothing but tinkling tassels when they walk –
tassels, earrings, phoenix hairpins.

The young girl and her wet nurse
have known death.
They are both searching for something leisuredly.
They face the midnight moon.
The girl is gentle and the light soft.
They float towards me
transforming the ordinary night
into a somnambulist trance.

Every night
the lantern floats over me.
Its owner wanders to the end of heaven,
his pace sometimes fast, sometimes slow.
No one can catch up with him,
the children grow up with him.

This is the story of the changing world and of the lantern.

If I sit on the floor
the chrysanthemum's shadow, the light's shadow and the shadows
of people

frighten me
and I sometimes slowly, sometimes quickly
make a silvery sound in my room.

If I sit on the bed
I can enjoy this sensation
while I gradually turn transparent,
gradually change colour.
All night I merge into mist
then rise into the air.

Jingan Village, June

after Zhai Yongming

Moonless night – the wind is high and boys practise killing.
Desire stirs in the wild wheatfield –
I can smell the drunkenness of the village.

For half a year I stare at the moon
until this twisted body of mine melts
and the spinning moon is a rusted hinge.
Everybody is drinking, having fun – no-one
notices me. At the garbage heap
I can feel an echo from the very heart of the earth.

A dusty farmer touches a fissure
in the old ebony table.
I think of legends from the great dynasties.
Tonight there'll be a lunar eclipse
and the farmer's wife will take a bath,
her eyes full of blind fear.

The veiled sky shivers and shapeshifts.
In the graveyard where ancestors lie
the baked mud walls crack open with dead eyes.
At dawn, tomb diggers will find
the coffins crawling with termites.
My body – all the bodies we are born with
decay in the dark and the light.

To an Ancient Cypress

after Du Fu

You stand in front of Kongming's shrine
with branches of green bronze, roots of rock.
Your hoary, rain-soaked bark spans forty metres,
your black crown pierces heaven.
The shrine is long forgotten
but you still draw worshippers who come to gaze as clouds
cling to you from the ghostly depths of Wu Gorge.
An icy moon rises over the snowy peaks perched on your fronds.
You are the road winding me back to my hut near Brocade River,
where ministers and warlords once sheltered in the same temple
and giant trees towered over the ancestral plain.
My derelict doors and windows reappear on your boughs.
Even dying, your snakelike trunk coils, encircling the earth,
while in your lonely heights force-ten gales howl.
Your power is supernatural – only the Change-Maker keeps you
                                                    upright.

If a vast hall should collapse and need new rafters,
the ten thousand oxen yoked to drag you
would turn and marvel at their mountainous load.
No carpenter could improve you since you already stun the world
though you have not yet reached your full girth.
Nothing could stop them felling you but who could wield the axe?
While phoenixes roost in your aromatic leaves
your bitter heart is riddled with termites.
Abandoned peoples, however neglected you feel, don't despair –
the greatest timber is always last to be used.

Ghost Sonatas

after Yang Lian

1. Ocean and River

Beyond the fence there's only ocean
but the cursed fish-star still sucks
more darkness from this moment.

Beyond the fence, surging waves
shake the sheer cliff.
Every night they rear higher.

Our bodies rhyme
with the pounding surf beneath our feet –
a blinding flood.

Every little hole is drenched.
Every breath is shoreless.
Our bodies' coastlines

wedge into each other.
We lick salt from the sea's skin.
In what century was that lamp among the rocks

lit? The sea swishes in our palms.
Memory has a river's tongue.
The cliff rises higher each night to collapse at the wings of birds.

Beyond the fence where we happened
to stop, we will always pause
to loose a black tide from our hearts.

2. The Music-Garden

Night's syringe
shoots a lethal dose
of darkness around our bed.

Carved by music,
the garden's contours are returning.
A gasping corolla bursts into colour.

Our wet crotches
wrench musical notes from the cassette. One after the other they
float up –
injected to the hilt. A candle flickers in deep space.

A ghost appears in the narrow pass.
It has chosen only the narrow pass of flesh
for its performance,

an endlessly recurring fragrance,
petal-trampling – all the seasons conjured in our room.
Every night the ghost ushers in

is huge as a constellation.
We press the rewind key for darkness to sing again
but nothing can be put off.

That which we water
the ghost passionately plucks, releasing us
from our scales. An improvised death renews our improvised life.

The Journey

after Yang Lian

1.
I wake when the wild goose calls, a cry
thousands of miles away, piercing
night's whirlpool.

The river turns. A parched child
thinks of a glass's inky rim
and wingtips sunk in cold crystal.

Night's hourglass anchors my house to the street.
After rain, tyres tear long bandages from the road.

I hear the boats in my body
jostling against each other, their keels fused.
When the wild goose cries, the city stuck to my eardrum
flies elsewhere, a geography light as a wreck.

2.
Water tells nothing.
The river turns. Wind rasps the hulls.
Rats love climbing the davit struts.
Rust sticks in my throat like a fish-bone.
Moonlight casts a lunar arc, painting a corpse's face,
quiet as a wooden womb thrown on the bank,
just by the lapping water, the gravel,
just by the rudder which has escaped all bearings among the stars,
the oars drawn in like tired questions
bound in a stranglehold around the axle.

Water tells nothing, but
on the water-surface the marina's glaze is fire-painted.
The clock ticks backwards –
what can a boat cradled by air remember
except water's embroidery,
except to be a bell, ringing to delete
my coiled ear, the ceaseless migrations.

But earth stalls.

The light-years woven around its nest
no longer know who sails on what river.
Water sinters into shatterproof porcelain
long broken, fissioning every night,
shattering my past, which so loves to invent.

Water tells nothing, therefore
in my abandoned boat, I can't raise the periscope
to peep at the sky where billions of orbits
clasp their lotus-suns. They close their corals, whisper
in a language which has no past tense, no nostalgia.
Their iron organs implode.
How long can we survive, when fish seek the poison in oxygen?
What more can we possibly find in an unblinking eye?
Dawn won't arrive. Dawn has swum elsewhere,
its beauty cuts me to the quick.

The wild geese's cries are an underwater co-ordinate.
What corpse can continue the journey ended last night?

3.
At the circle's centre, a text secretly watches me
draft another page.
My bed circles – floating in a ghost script
revealed then unravelled by water.

Did the wild geese really cry, or is this night too adrift
for their arched and chopped necks?
The more afraid I am to listen, the easier they're summoned.

Their call transforms the landscape; darkness
transforms my flesh;
the city's hydromechanics splash out a branch of peach-blossom.
A hammering heartbeat still withholds the horizon.

My mind is a starry sky; my bed-edge
a starboard –
a scream locked in a raindrop, the pull of dreams
longing for each other over thousands of miles
all in the circle, driven out by what isn't yet written

only to circle back to here.

Acknowledgements

Acknowledgements are due to the editors of the following publications in which some of these poems first appeared: *In the Red, Fragments from the Dark, Literary Imagination* (US), *Magma, Manhattan Review* (US), *Modern Poetry in Translation, New Welsh Review, Pendulum, Poetry International* (US), *Poetry London, Poetry Monthly* (China), *Poetry Review, Poetry Wales, Pratik* (Nepal), *Quadrant* (Australia), *Resurgence, Rialto, Skein of Geese: poems from the 100 Poets Gathering at StAnza 2007, Stimulus Respond, Women's Work: Modern Women Poets Writing in English.*

New Welsh Review commissioned 'The Bee Mother' for a collaboration with Magnum photographer David Hurn. *Poetry Review* commissioned 'Osprey Nests' for the Prose Sculpture Poem feature, and is drawn from David Gessner's *Return of the Osprey*, Ballantine Books 2001, pp.35–6. The Royal Watercolour Society commissioned 'Night Boat on Galilee' for their exhibition *Poets and Painters* in November 2008. 'Exiled Elm' was commissioned by the sculptor Jilly Sutton for her exhibition *The Family Tree Show* at the Rebecca Hossack gallery, March 2009.

I am grateful to Arts Council England for two awards, the first of which enabled me to take part in the Poet to Poet translation project in China and Scotland in 2005, and to Julian Forrester of Cove Park Artists Centre, Polly Clark, and Zhang Wei of Wansongpu Writers Centre. The second award was to complete this collection and travel to Nepal in 2007. I am grateful to the Society of Authors for an Author's Foundation grant and to the Royal Literary Fund for a Fellowship at Middlesex University 2007–9. Thanks to Yuyutsu R.D. Sharma for the Annapurna trek, and to Yang Lian for the Yellow Mountain Poetry Festival in China and the UK in 2007 and 2008. I would like to thank the British Council for inviting me to their New Silk Route project in Almaty and to Literature Across Frontiers and Helicon for inviting me to Israel. These journeys made many of these poems possible.

Warm thanks to Zhai Yongming and Zhou Zan for working with me on translations of their poems and for permission to include them in this collection, to Yang Lian for his help translating his poems which will appear in his new collection *Lee Valley Poems* (Bloodaxe, 2009).

'Treesitter' is dedicated to Julia Butterfly Hill, who treesat and saved the coast redwood Luna. 'Redwood Canopy Explorer' is dedicated to Steve Sillett for his explorations of coast redwood reiterated canopies. 'Nature Singer' is dedicated to the nature singer Charles Kellogg (1868–1949). Finally, thanks to Amy Wack, and special thanks to my husband Brian Fraser my first reader and companion in Nepal, Humboldt Redwoods State Park and Redwood National Parks, California.